My Snowman

Heather Hammonds

Contents

Snow	**2**
My Snowman	**8**
The Sun	**10**
Where Is My Snowman?	**14**
Glossary	**16**

Snow

Look at the **snow**.

The snow is on the trees.

The snow is on Mum.
The snow is on me.

Here are

some little **snowballs.**

I can run in the snow.
I can play in the snow.

My Snowman

This is a big **snowman.**

Here are two eyes for the snowman.

The Sun

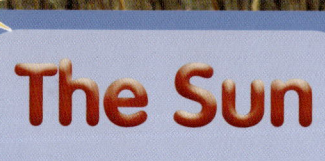

The sun is shining today.

The sun is on the snow.

The sun is on us.

The sun is
on my snowman, too.

Look at my snowman!

Where Is My Snowman?

I looked for my snowman.

My snowman is not here.

I can see some snow on the grass.

Where is my snowman?

Glossary

snow

snowballs